Things to Know When Preparing for a Cybersecurity Analyst Interview

Table of Contents

Introduction

In today's world where technology is rapidly advancing, cybersecurity has become a necessity. Cybersecurity Analysts are the people who ensure that an organization's system is secure from unauthorized access and threats. This job is highly demanding and requires a great deal of knowledge and expertise in the subject matter.

The field of cybersecurity is ever-evolving, and even the most experienced cybersecurity analysts need to keep themselves updated with the latest trends and technologies. Preparing for a job interview in this field can be daunting, and it can be difficult to know where to begin. This book has been written to help aspiring cybersecurity analysts prepare for their interview by providing them with a comprehensive list of terms and definitions that will help them understand the cybersecurity concepts better.

Access Controls

A security technique that restricts access to confidential information, systems, or resources to authorized personnel only. Access control is a critical aspect of cybersecurity as it ensures that important data and resources are only accessed by those who have the necessary authorization level. There are several types of access controls including mandatory access control, discretionary access control, and role-based access control, each with its unique approach to controlling access.

Active Directory

A directory service that authenticates and authorizes users and computers in a Windows domain network. Active Directory is Microsoft's proprietary directory service used by system administrators to centralize and manage network resources, including the management of users, computers, and other resources such as servers, printers, and software applications.

Adversary

An individual, group, or organization that actively seeks to compromise or exploit an information system or network. Adversaries can include hackers, cybercriminals, nation-states, or insiders with malicious intent. Understanding the types of adversaries and their tactics is critical for cybersecurity defense.

Anomaly Detection

A technique used in cybersecurity to identify deviations from normal system behavior or patterns. Anomaly detection is a critical component of intrusion detection and prevention systems as it enables security personnel to detect and respond to potential security breaches or malicious activity. Techniques used for anomaly detection include statistical analysis, machine learning, and artificial intelligence.

Application Security

A critical component of cybersecurity that involves secure coding practices, testing, and software development methodologies to ensure that applications and software are free of vulnerabilities that can be exploited by attackers.

Asset Management

The process of identifying, categorizing, and maintaining a record of an organization's hardware, software, and other assets. Asset management is essential for cybersecurity as it helps organizations have complete visibility over their IT infrastructure and maintain an inventory of devices, software, and applications for effective security management.

Attack Surface

The total number of vulnerabilities, configurations, and access points that can be exploited by attackers. The attack surface is the sum of all potential vulnerabilities that can be exploited by attackers to gain unauthorized access to a system or application. Evaluating the attack surface is critical for cybersecurity as it helps organizations understand the level of risk associated with their IT infrastructure.

Audit Trails

A record of all events and activities that occur within an information system, including access attempts, changes, and system interactions. Audit trails are critical for cybersecurity as they enable security personnel to detect unauthorized access attempts, security breaches, or other malicious activities.

Authentication

The process of verifying the identity of a user, system, or device. Authentication is an essential element of cybersecurity as it ensures that only authorized users can access resources. Authentication techniques include passwords, tokens, biometrics, digital certificates, and other multifactor authentication techniques.

Authorization

The process of granting access to a user, system, or device based on their level of clearance, permissions, or privileges. Authorization is critical for cybersecurity as it ensures that only authorized persons can access resources, systems, or applications, and those privileges can be revoked when necessary.

Backup and disaster recovery

A plan and practice of regularly backing up all critical digital assets and establishing a recovery strategy in case of a cyber attack or natural disaster. This includes regularly backing up data, testing recovery processes, and ensuring that backups are stored securely and offsite. A sound backup and disaster recovery plan can help organizations quickly recover from cyber attacks and avoid significant data losses.

Baseline

A benchmark against which future measurements or changes are compared. In cybersecurity, a baseline can be used to establish a standard for normal network traffic, user behavior, system configuration, or any other measurable aspect. This allows cybersecurity professionals to detect anomalies or deviations from the baseline, indicating potential security incidents.

Black hat

A hacker or cybercriminal who uses their technical skills for illegal or malicious purposes. Black hat hackers may steal sensitive data, launch cyber attacks, or engage in other illegal activities. Black hat hacking is often considered a form of cybercrime and is punishable by law.

Blue team

A group of professionals responsible for defending an organization's digital assets against cyber threats. Blue team is often a part of a larger cybersecurity team and is focused primarily on ensuring the security of the organization's network infrastructure. Members of a blue team are responsible for monitoring network activities, detecting and responding to security incidents, and implementing security controls to prevent future attacks.

Botnet

A network of computers or devices that are infected with malware and controlled by a remote attacker. Botnets are often used in cyber attacks, allowing the attacker to remotely control a large number of compromised devices to conduct various malicious activities, such as distributing spam emails, launching DDoS attacks, or stealing sensitive data.

Breach

An unauthorized access to or acquisition of an organization's digital assets, such as customer data or intellectual property, by an attacker. Breaches can happen due to a variety of reasons, including weak passwords, unpatched software vulnerabilities, or social engineering techniques. Breaches can cause significant damage to an organization's reputation and finances.

Bridge

A device that connects two or more networks, allowing them to communicate and share resources. Bridges can be physical devices or software programs and are often used to extend the reach of a network or segment it for security purposes. Bridges should be properly configured and secured to prevent unauthorized access or attacks.

Bring Your Own Device (BYOD)

A policy in which employees are allowed to use their personal devices, such as smartphones or laptops, for work purposes. BYOD policies can increase productivity and employee satisfaction but also pose cybersecurity risks, as personal devices may not have the same security controls as company-owned devices. Effective BYOD policies must balance the advantages and disadvantages and implement appropriate security measures to mitigate risks.

Bug bounty

A program in which organizations offer rewards to individuals or groups who find and report security vulnerabilities in their systems. Bug bounty programs are increasingly popular among companies, as they can help identify and remediate security issues before attackers exploit them. Successful bug bounty programs require clear guidelines, fair rewards, and efficient vulnerability management processes.

Business continuity

The ability of an organization to maintain essential functions and services during and after a disruption, such as a cyber attack or natural disaster. Business continuity planning includes identifying critical services, developing contingency plans, and establishing communication and recovery procedures. Business continuity planning is crucial for minimizing the impact of disruptions and ensuring that the organization can recover quickly.

Compliance

Compliance refers to an organization's adherence to industry standards, laws, and regulations. Cybersecurity Analysts need to ensure that their organization's systems and processes comply with industry standards to minimize the risk of cyber attacks and data breaches.

Configuration Management

Configuration Management refers to the process of managing the hardware and software configuration of an organization's systems to ensure they are secure and compliant. Cybersecurity Analysts need to manage and maintain the configuration of an organization's systems to reduce the risk of security breaches and attacks.

Cryptography

Cryptography is the practice of securing communication from unauthorized access by converting it into a code. Cybersecurity Analysts need to have a thorough understanding of cryptography to protect data transmitted over networks. They also need to be familiar with encryption and decryption techniques to protect sensitive information against hacking and unauthorized access.

Cyber Incident Response

Cyber Incident Response is the process of quickly identifying and responding to a cyber attack or security breach. Cybersecurity Analysts need to have a well-defined incident response plan in place and be ready to take swift action to mitigate the impact of an attack.

Cyber Threat Intelligence

Cyber Threat Intelligence can be defined as the collection, evaluation, and analysis of data related to an adversary's capabilities, intentions, and activities. This information can be used to predict and prevent cyber attacks. Cybersecurity Analysts use Cyber Threat Intelligence to stay up-to-date on the latest cyber threats and to identify potential vulnerabilities in their organization's systems.

Cybersecurity Awareness Training

Cybersecurity Awareness Training is the process of educating employees and other stakeholders on the importance of cybersecurity and how to prevent cyber attacks. Cybersecurity Analysts need to be involved in developing and delivering cybersecurity awareness training programs to minimize the risk of human error leading to security breaches.

Cybersecurity Framework

A Cybersecurity Framework is a set of guidelines and best practices designed to help organizations manage cybersecurity risks. Cybersecurity Analysts need to be familiar with different frameworks such as NIST, CIS, and ISO/IEC 27001 to help their organizations comply with industry standards and regulations.

Cybersecurity Governance

Cybersecurity Governance refers to the policies, procedures, and controls put in place to manage an organization's cybersecurity program. Cybersecurity Analysts need to help organizations establish proper governance structures to ensure that their cybersecurity programs are effective and efficient.

Cybersecurity Monitoring

Cybersecurity Monitoring is the process of continuously monitoring an organization's systems and networks for potential security incidents. Cybersecurity Analysts need to use sophisticated tools such as Intrusion Detection Systems (IDS) and Security Information and Event Management (SIEM) systems to identify and mitigate potential threats.

Cybersecurity Risk Assessment

A Cybersecurity Risk Assessment is a process of identifying, analyzing, and evaluating potential risks that could impact an organization's systems and data. Cybersecurity Analysts need to be adept at performing risk assessments and creating strategies to mitigate these risks.

Email Phishing

Email phishing is a cyber attack that involves sending fraudulent emails that appear to be from a legitimate source, in order to trick recipients into revealing sensitive information. This type of attack is often used to steal passwords and financial information.

Encryption

Encryption is the process of converting plain text or data into a code or cypher that cannot be easily read by unauthorized users. It is used to protect sensitive data such as passwords and credit card information from cyber attackers.

Encryption Algorithm

An encryption algorithm is a set of instructions used to encrypt and decrypt data. It is used to protect sensitive data from cyber attacks by converting it into a code or cipher that is difficult to decipher without the correct encryption key.

Encryption Key

An encryption key is a piece of information used to encrypt and decrypt data. It is usually a complex string of characters that is required to access encrypted data.

Endpoint Detection and Response (EDR)

EDR is a security system that monitors endpoint devices such as laptops and smartphones for potential security threats. It includes features such as behavioral analysis, threat hunting, and incident response.

Endpoint Security

Endpoint security refers to the security system used to protect networked devices, including laptops, smartphones, and tablets, from cyber attacks. It includes methods such as firewalls, antivirus software, and intrusion detection systems.

Ethical Hacking

Ethical hacking is the practice of testing a company's computer systems and network for vulnerabilities in order to identify potential security threats. It is done with the permission of the company and is used to improve the company's overall security.

Event Correlation

Event correlation is the process of analyzing multiple events and identifying patterns or relationships between them. It is used to detect and respond to security threats and to identify potential security breaches.

Event Logging

Event logging is the practice of recording all events that occur on a network or computer system, including login attempts, file system access, and software installations. This information is used to monitor for potential security breaches and to investigate incidents.

Exploit

An exploit is a piece of software or code that takes advantage of a vulnerability or weakness in a computer system or network. Attackers use exploits to gain unauthorized access to a system or to crash it.

False Positive

An alert generated by a security system that incorrectly identifies benign activity as malicious or threatening.

File Integrity Monitoring

A cybersecurity practice that involves monitoring and analyzing files to detect any unauthorized changes, deletions, or corruption of data.

Filtering

A process of selectively allowing or blocking network traffic based on specific criteria, such as source address, destination address, or protocol.

Firewall

A network security system that monitors and controls incoming and outgoing network traffic based on predetermined security rules.

Firmware

Software that is embedded in a hardware device, such as a router or printer, and is responsible for controlling the device's operation.

Flood Attack

A type of denial-of-service (DoS) attack, where a large number of requests are sent to a server or network in an attempt to overwhelm and disrupt its services.

Forensic Analysis

A process of collecting, analyzing, and preserving electronic data in a way that maintains the integrity of the evidence for use in a court of law or an internal investigation.

Frequency Analysis

A technique that involves analyzing the frequency at which certain events occur to identify patterns or anomalies that may indicate a security threat.

Full-Disk Encryption

An encryption technique where an entire hard drive or storage device is encrypted, protecting all data on the device from unauthorized access or theft.

Fuzz Testing

A technique used to find security vulnerabilities in software by testing it with random and invalid inputs.

Gap analysis

An assessment that identifies the differences between an organization's current cybersecurity posture and its desired state. It helps prioritize areas for improvement and guides decision-making for resource allocation.

Gateway

A network component that connects two different networks and controls traffic flow between them. It is often used to protect internal networks from external threats. A cybersecurity analyst should be familiar with the different types of gateways and their functions.

GDPR (General Data Protection Regulation)

A regulation implemented by the European Union that regulates the collection, storage, and use of personal data. It applies to all companies that process the personal data of EU residents. A cybersecurity analyst should understand GDPR and its implications for the organization's data protection practices.

Golden image

A standardized image of a system that is used to deploy multiple instances of the same configuration. It ensures consistency and reduces the risk of misconfiguration. A cybersecurity analyst should understand golden images and how to secure them.

Good faith vulnerability testing

A type of security testing that is conducted with the goal of improving security and identifying vulnerabilities for remediation. It is different from malicious hacking, where the goal is to exploit vulnerabilities for personal gain. A cybersecurity analyst should understand good faith vulnerability testing and the ethical considerations associated with it.

Governance

The processes, policies, and procedures that guide an organization in achieving its goals and objectives while managing risks and complying with laws and regulations. A cybersecurity analyst should understand the governance structure of the organization and how it impacts cybersecurity decisions.

GRC (governance, risk management, and compliance)

A framework that helps organizations manage and mitigate risks, comply with regulations, and achieve their objectives. A cybersecurity analyst should be familiar with GRC frameworks and how they impact the organization's cybersecurity posture.

Grey box testing

A type of security testing that simulates an attacker with limited knowledge of the system being tested. It helps identify vulnerabilities that may not be obvious to an outside attacker but are accessible to someone with limited information. A cybersecurity analyst should understand grey box testing and how to use it in a comprehensive testing program.

Greylisting

A spam filtering technique that temporarily rejects email messages from unknown senders. It helps reduce the amount of spam that reaches the user's inbox. A cybersecurity analyst should be familiar with greylisting and its effectiveness in reducing spam.

Group policy

A set of rules that controls the behavior and configuration of computers and users in an Active Directory domain. A cybersecurity analyst should have a strong understanding of how to configure group policies to enforce security settings and restrictions.

Hacker mindset

A way of thinking like an attacker to discover vulnerabilities before they can be exploited. This mindset involves understanding the motivations and methods of hackers, as well as constantly searching for weaknesses in the system. Cybersecurity analysts with a hacker mindset can think creatively and develop effective strategies to protect against future attacks.

Hardening

The process of configuring a system to be more secure against potential threats. This involves disabling unnecessary services and features, as well as implementing security controls such as firewalls and antivirus software. Hardening can help to reduce the attack surface of a system, making it less vulnerable to potential exploits.

Hashing

A technique for securely storing and transmitting data. It involves taking a block of data and running it through a cryptographic hash function to produce a fixed-length string of characters, known as a hash or message digest. If even a single character of the original data is changed, the resulting hash will be completely different. Hashing is often used to verify the integrity of data, as well as to store passwords securely.

Header

The portion of a network packet or protocol message that contains information about the data being transmitted. Headers typically include information such as the source and destination IP addresses, port numbers, and protocol type. Cybersecurity analysts use headers to identify potential threats, such as packets with suspicious source IP addresses or unusual protocol behavior.

Heuristics

A method of detecting new and unknown malware based on behavioral patterns. Heuristics involves examining the code of a potentially harmful program and allowing it to run in a sandbox environment, where its behavior can be monitored. By analyzing the way the program interacts with the system, heuristics can identify potential threats that may not be caught by traditional signature-based approaches.

Honeypot

A decoy system designed to attract and detect hackers. It is essentially a trap that appears vulnerable to attackers, but is actually closely monitored by cybersecurity professionals. Honeypots can be used for research purposes, as well as to divert attention away from real systems and gather information on potential threats.

Host-based intrusion detection system (HIDS)

A type of intrusion detection system that monitors activity on a single host or endpoint. HIDS can detect malicious activity such as file modifications, unauthorized logins, and suspicious network connections. It can also provide alerts and notifications to security personnel, allowing them to respond quickly to potential threats.

HTTP header injection

A type of web-based attack that involves inserting malicious code into an HTTP header. This can allow an attacker to execute arbitrary code on a vulnerable server, steal sensitive data, or redirect users to malicious sites. Cybersecurity analysts must be able to detect and prevent HTTP header injections to protect against these attacks.

Hybrid analysis

A method of malware analysis that combines both static and dynamic analysis techniques. Hybrid analysis involves examining the code of a program in a sandbox environment, as well as examining its behavior as it runs. This approach can help to identify both known and unknown threats, and can provide a more comprehensive understanding of how a particular malware sample works.

Hybrid cloud

A cloud computing environment that combines elements of public and private cloud. In a hybrid cloud, certain applications and data are stored in a private cloud, while others are housed in a public cloud. This approach allows organizations to take advantage of the scalability and cost savings of public cloud while maintaining control and security over sensitive data.

Identity Management

The process of managing and controlling user access to an organization's information assets, including data, systems, and applications. This includes the implementation of authentication and authorization processes, as well as user account management practices. A strong knowledge of identity management techniques is essential for a cybersecurity analyst, as it is imperative to control who has access to sensitive information and to ensure that only authorized users can access it.

Incident Response

The process of responding to a cyber attack or security breach in a systematic and planned manner. It involves identifying the scope of the attack, containing it, analyzing its impact, and then implementing measures to restore normal operations. As a cybersecurity analyst, it is crucial to have a solid understanding of incident response processes, methods, and techniques, including tools such as intrusion detection systems and forensic analysis tools.

Information Security Policy

A set of guidelines that defines an organization's rules and procedures for protecting its information assets. These policies can include password requirements, access controls, data classification methods, and incident response procedures. During a cybersecurity analyst interview, it is important to be able to discuss information security policies and identify how they are implemented and enforced within an organization.

Infrastructure Security

The protection of an organization's information technology infrastructure, including networks, hardware, and software, against unauthorized access, modification, or destruction. This can include implementing firewalls, intrusion detection and prevention systems, and vulnerability management processes. As an analyst, understanding infrastructure security measures and best practices is essential to ensuring the safety and security of an organization's information.

Insider Threat

The risk of sensitive information being compromised by employees or other internal parties who have authorized access. An insider threat can occur due to intentional or accidental actions, including human error or malicious intent. As a cybersecurity analyst, it is important to understand the insider threat and be able to identify risks and implement policies and procedures to mitigate them.

Intrusion Detection

The process of detecting unauthorized and malicious activity within an organization's network or system. This involves continuously monitoring for indicators of compromise, such as unusual network traffic patterns or system behavior. Being familiar with intrusion detection systems and techniques is essential for a cybersecurity analyst, as it is crucial to be able to detect and respond to security incidents quickly and effectively.

Java

Java is a high-level, object-oriented programming language that is widely used in enterprise applications. Cybersecurity analysts may encounter Java-based applications and need to understand the security implications of running or interacting with them. Familiarity with Java programming language and concepts is an added advantage.

JavaScript

JavaScript is a programming language that is mostly used for creating interactive web pages and web applications. In the context of cybersecurity, JavaScript is often used to create malicious code that can be injected into web pages, which can lead to data breaches and other cyber attacks. Understanding JavaScript and its potential security risks is important for cybersecurity analysts.

Jira

Jira is a popular project management tool that is widely used in the software development industry. It helps teams to plan, track, and manage their work by providing a centralized platform. Cybersecurity analysts may use Jira to track and manage cybersecurity incidents and vulnerabilities, assign tasks to team members, and monitor progress.

Job Description

A Job Description is a document that outlines the duties, responsibilities, and qualifications required for a specific job. When preparing for a Cybersecurity Analyst interview, reviewing the Job Description can give an idea of what skills the company is seeking. Analyzing the Job Description will allow the candidate to tailor their answers and explain how their past experiences make them an ideal fit for the position. Candidates can also use the Job Description as a guide to prepare for interview questions.

Job Experience

When preparing for a Cybersecurity Analyst interview, it's essential to reflect on one's past job experience to highlight relevant skills and experiences that make the candidate suitable for the position. Cybersecurity Analysts need to demonstrate their experience with network security, incident response, threat intelligence, vulnerability assessment, and penetration testing. Being able to provide concrete examples of past experience will help to set the right impression during an interview.

JSON

JSON stands for JavaScript Object Notation and is a lightweight, text-based data format that is often used to transmit data between applications. Cybersecurity analysts may encounter JSON files when analyzing network traffic or system logs. Understanding how to read and interpret JSON files is an important skill for cybersecurity analysts.

Jumbo Frame

Jumbo frames are Ethernet frames that exceed the standard Maximum Transmission Unit (MTU) of 1500 bytes. Jumbo frames can be used to increase network performance but may also introduce cybersecurity risks. Cybersecurity analysts may need to understand how Jumbo Frames work and how to secure networks that use them.

Jump Box

A Jump Box, also known as a Bastion host, is a secure computer that is used to access and manage a network securely. It acts as a gateway to the network and allows authorized users to access the system without exposing it to external threats. Cybersecurity analysts may interact with Jump Boxes when accessing remote systems or providing remote support.

Juniper Networks

Juniper Networks is a company that provides networking and cybersecurity products and services. Their products range from network devices, routers, switches, and security devices. Familiarity with Juniper Networks products and services is valuable for Cybersecurity Analysts.

Jupyter Notebook

The Jupyter Notebook is an open-source web application that allows users to create and share documents with live code, interactive widgets, visualizations, and text. This tool is widely used in the field of data science and can be used by Cybersecurity Analyst to do data mining, exploratory data analysis, and data visualization. Familiarity with Jupyter Notebook is an added advantage for Cybersecurity Analysts.

Kali Linux

Kali Linux is a widely-used Linux distribution that is used by cybersecurity professionals to perform security assessments and penetration testing. It comes pre-installed with several powerful tools that can be used to identify vulnerabilities in the target system. A cybersecurity analyst should be familiar with Kali Linux and its various tools to perform security testing effectively.

Kerberos

Kerberos is a network authentication protocol that is used to provide secure communication between two endpoints. It operates on the basis of tickets that are issued by a central authentication server, which holds the user's credentials. These tickets are then verified by application servers before granting access to the user. A cybersecurity analyst should be proficient in Kerberos and its associated technologies to ensure that secure authentication mechanisms are in place.

Kernel

The kernel is the core component of an operating system. It provides low-level access to the hardware and manages system resources. A cybersecurity analyst should have knowledge of kernel-level vulnerabilities and techniques used to exploit them.

Key management

Key management involves the secure storage, distribution, and usage of cryptographic keys. It is a critical aspect of ensuring the confidentiality and integrity of data. A cybersecurity analyst should have knowledge of various key management techniques and best practices to ensure that the organization's data remains secure.

Key pairs

A key pair is a set of two cryptographic keys that are used to encrypt and decrypt data. It comprises of a public key, which is shared with the world, and a private key, which is kept secret. These keys play a crucial role in digital signatures, secure email communication, and confidentiality of data. A cybersecurity analyst needs to have a clear understanding of key pairs and their applications to ensure that the organization's data is protected from unauthorized access.

Kill chain

The kill chain refers to the sequence of events that an attacker follows to launch an attack successfully. It typically includes the following stages

Knowledge of cryptography

Cryptography is the science of secure communication. It involves the use of mathematical algorithms to ensure confidentiality, integrity, and authenticity of data. A cybersecurity analyst should have a good understanding of various cryptographic concepts and techniques such as symmetric key cryptography, asymmetric key cryptography, encryption, and decryption.

Knowledge of network protocols

A cybersecurity analyst should have a deep understanding of network protocols, including TCP/IP, DNS, HTTP, FTP, and SSH. This knowledge helps to identify network anomalies and suspicious traffic patterns that may indicate malicious activity. Understanding network protocols is an essential skill that every cybersecurity analyst should possess.

Knowledge of operating systems

A cybersecurity analyst should have a strong understanding of the operating systems used within the organization. This knowledge is essential for identifying vulnerabilities in the system and implementing appropriate security controls. In addition, it helps to ensure that the system remains configured in a secure manner.

LAN (Local Area Network)

A network that connects devices within a limited geographic area, such as a building or campus. Cybersecurity analysts may need to secure LANs against unauthorized access and monitor network traffic for signs of a security breach.

Layered Security

A security approach that involves using multiple security controls to protect computer systems or networks. This can include firewalls, intrusion prevention systems, antivirus software, and access controls. A cybersecurity analyst may recommend implementing layered security to reduce the risk of an attack succeeding.

LDAP (Lightweight Directory Access Protocol)

A protocol used to access and manage directory services on a network. Cybersecurity analysts may use LDAP to manage user access, authentication, and authorization on a network.

Least Privilege

A principle of cybersecurity that states that users and processes should only have access to the resources necessary to perform their tasks. This can reduce the risk of an attacker gaining access to sensitive information or systems. A cybersecurity analyst may recommend implementing least privilege access controls as part of a security strategy.

Linux

An open-source operating system used in many server environments. A cybersecurity analyst may need to know how to secure and configure Linux systems, as they are often used in web servers and critical infrastructure systems.

Logging

The process of recording events that happen on a computer system or network. Cybersecurity analysts use logs to audit activities and investigate security incidents on a system. Log files can contain information about user activities, network traffic, and system events.

Malware

Malware is any software designed to harm or compromise computer systems, networks, or devices. Common types of malware include viruses, trojan horses, ransomware, and spyware. As a cybersecurity analyst, understanding the characteristics and behavior of different types of malware is crucial in detecting and mitigating cyber threats.

Mitigation

Mitigation refers to the process of reducing the impact of a security incident or potential threat. This can be done by applying security controls, implementing security best practices, or conducting risk assessments to identify vulnerabilities and prioritize remediation efforts. As a cybersecurity analyst, having a strong understanding of mitigation strategies is important in developing effective security protocols and incident response plans.

Multi-factor authentication

Multi-factor authentication is a security measure that requires users to provide multiple types of authentication, such as a password and a biometric factor, to access a network or application. This provides an extra layer of security to prevent unauthorized access, especially in cases where passwords may be compromised. As a cybersecurity analyst, understanding multi-factor authentication systems and their implementation is important in maintaining robust security standards.

National Security Agency (NSA)

A U.S. intelligence agency responsible for collecting and analyzing foreign signals intelligence. The NSA also has a role in cybersecurity, developing and implementing secure communication protocols and other defensive measures. Cybersecurity analysts should be aware of the NSA's role in protecting national security and the potential implications for their organization.

Nessus

A vulnerability scanner used to identify potential weaknesses in computer systems and networks. It scans for known vulnerabilities in operating systems, software applications, and other network devices. Cybersecurity analysts often rely on vulnerability scanners like Nessus to identify potential security risks and prioritize remediation efforts.

Network Access Control (NAC)

A security solution that controls access to network resources based on predetermined policies. NAC solutions can verify the identity of users and devices before granting access to the network, and can enforce security policies such as antivirus and firewall protection. Cybersecurity analysts must understand how NAC solutions work and how to configure them to effectively secure their organization's networks.

Network Security

The practice of securing computer networks from unauthorized access or damage. This includes implementing firewalls, antivirus software, intrusion detection and prevention systems, and other security measures. Cybersecurity analysts must have extensive knowledge of network security to effectively protect their organization's systems and data.

Network Segmentation

The process of dividing a computer network into smaller subnetworks, called segments, to improve overall security. Segmented networks can help contain security breaches by limiting the spread of malware and other attacks. This is important for cybersecurity analysts to understand as it allows them to identify potential vulnerabilities and prioritize security measures for each segment.

Network Traffic Analysis

The process of monitoring and analyzing network traffic to identify and respond to potential security threats. This includes analyzing network packets, logs and other data to identify patterns or anomalies that may indicate an attack or breach. Cybersecurity analysts must be skilled in network traffic analysis to quickly detect and respond to security incidents.

Next-Generation Firewall (NGFW)

A firewall solution that integrates traditional firewall functionality with additional security features such as intrusion prevention, application control, and advanced malware protection. NGFWs provide more comprehensive threat protection than traditional firewalls and are becoming increasingly important in the cybersecurity landscape. Cybersecurity analysts should be familiar with NGFW technology and its features.

NIST Cybersecurity Framework

A framework developed by the National Institute of Standards and Technology (NIST) that provides a common language for managing cybersecurity risk. It consist of five core functions

NIST Special Publication 800-53

A framework developed by NIST that outlines security and privacy controls for federal information systems and organizations. This framework is commonly used in the public sector and by organizations that work with the U.S. government. Cybersecurity analysts should be familiar with this framework and its requirements.

Non-Repudiation

The ability to prove the origin and integrity of a message or transaction. This is important for cybersecurity analysts as it ensures that digital signatures and transactions cannot be disputed or repudiated, providing a reliable method of validation.

OAuth (Open Authorization)

A protocol used for authorization to access protected resources on behalf of a user. Cybersecurity Analysts should be familiar with OAuth to identify and prevent common attacks, such as OAuth phishing and authorization code injection, that can compromise user accounts and data.

One-Time Password (OTP)

A unique numerical code that is generated for a single login session or transaction. OTPs are commonly used in two-factor authentication to provide an additional layer of security beyond traditional username and password authentication. Cybersecurity Analysts should be knowledgeable about OTPs to ensure these systems are secure and not easily bypassed by attackers.

Onion Routing

A technique that uses a series of interconnected servers to create a private and anonymous network. The Tor network is a commonly used onion routing system that prevents anyone from monitoring a user's online activity, making it difficult for Cybersecurity Analysts to detect and prevent malicious activities originating from these networks.

Onion Services

Services hosted on the Tor network that can only be accessed through the Tor browser. These services are commonly used by malicious actors to hide their activities from law enforcement and Cybersecurity Analysts. Therefore, it is important for Cybersecurity Analysts to be familiar with onion services and the tools used to detect and prevent malicious activities originating from these systems.

Open-Source Intelligence (OSINT)

A collection and analysis of publicly available information to gather intelligence and relevant data for cybersecurity investigations. Cybersecurity Analysts use OSINT tools and techniques to identify potential threats, such as malicious actors, stolen credentials, and phishing sites, to protect their organization's network and data.

OpenVAS (Open Vulnerability Assessment System)

An open-source vulnerability scanner used to detect and report vulnerabilities in network and application security. Cybersecurity Analysts should be knowledgeable about open-source tools like OpenVAS to conduct comprehensive security assessments and prevent potential exploits and attacks.

Operating System (OS)

A program that manages computer hardware and software resources and provides common services for computer programs. Cybersecurity Analysts should have a solid understanding of different operating systems, such as Windows, Linux, and macOS, to identify and defend against various security threats targeting these systems.

Opt-In

A consent mechanism that requires explicit action from the user to permit the collection and use of their personal data. Cybersecurity Analysts should be knowledgeable about opt-in policies and ensure that the organization's data collection and processing activities comply with local regulations and privacy laws.

OSCP (Offensive Security Certified Professional)

A certification offered by Offensive Security that measures practical knowledge of penetration testing methodologies and techniques. Cybersecurity Analysts who hold the OSCP certification are highly sought after by employers for their advanced skills in identifying and exploiting vulnerabilities in network and application security.

Out-of-Band (OOB) Management

A management technique that uses a separate communication channel, such as a modem or serial cable, to access and manage network devices. Cybersecurity Analysts should be knowledgeable about OOB management techniques to prevent attackers from gaining unauthorized access to critical network infrastructure.

Packet Filtering

A technique used by firewalls to examine incoming and outgoing network traffic, based on predetermined rules to allow or deny access. Packet filters can be used to block unwanted traffic and help mitigate potential security risks.

Password Policy

A set of rules and guidelines that determine how users must create and manage their passwords. Password policies are important for ensuring that passwords are secure and difficult to guess or hack, thereby improving the overall security of a system.

Patch Management

The process of identifying, acquiring, testing, and installing patches for software vulnerabilities on a regular basis to improve system performance and reduce security risks. This process helps to keep software up-to-date, secure, and stable.

Payload

A component of malware that delivers the malicious activity, such as performing unauthorized actions, stealing data, or opening a backdoor on the target system. The payload is often the ultimate goal of an attacker and can cause significant damage once executed.

Penetration Testing

A method of assessing the security of an information system by repeatedly attempting to exploit the vulnerabilities present in the system. Penetration testing is done to identify the loopholes in the security system and to make recommendations to strengthen them.

PGP (Pretty Good Privacy)

A widely used encryption software that provides cryptographic privacy and authentication for data communication, email, and file storage. PGP is used to encrypt files, messages, and emails to ensure the data is secure and confidential, and only accessible to authorized users.

Phishing

An attempt to gain sensitive information, such as usernames and passwords, by masquerading as a trustworthy entity in an electronic communication. This can be done through messages, emails or website links, where attackers use social engineering to manipulate individuals into providing personal information.

Port Scanning

A technique used for probing a network to identify which services are running and to detect vulnerabilities that may be present. This method can help identify open ports that can be exploited by attackers to gain unauthorized access to the system.

Privilege Escalation

A method used by attackers to gain access to systems or resources that are unauthorized by increasing their level of access beyond their current privileges. This can be done by exploiting vulnerabilities within the system, providing access to sensitive data and resources.

Protocol

A set of rules and standards that govern how data is transmitted over a network. Different protocols ensure the proper functioning and security of the communication, such as HTTPS for secure web browsing or SSH for secure remote access. Understanding protocols is important for identifying potential network security issues and designing secure networks.

QEMU

QEMU is a virtualization platform that allows the creation and management of virtual machines. Cybersecurity Analysts may be asked about their experience using QEMU and other virtualization platforms, as well as their knowledge of best practices for securing virtual environments.

QoS

Quality of Service (QoS) is a network management technique that prioritizes certain types of traffic over others, to ensure that critical traffic (such as voice or video) receives the necessary resources and bandwidth. Cybersecurity Analysts may be asked about their experience with QoS, and their ability to design and implement QoS policies that improve network performance and security.

Quadrant model

The quadrant model is a way of visualizing risk management strategies. The model divides risks into four quadrants based on their likelihood and impact, with the idea being that risks in the top left quadrant (high impact, high likelihood) require the most attention and mitigation efforts. Cybersecurity Analysts may be asked about their experience with the quadrant model, and their ability to use it to inform risk management strategies.

Qualitative analysis

Qualitative analysis is a type of investigative approach that focuses on understanding the "why" and "how" behind a particular phenomenon, as opposed to simply measuring and quantifying it. During an interview, you may be asked about your experience conducting qualitative analysis, and your ability to apply those skills to investigating security incidents or analyzing threat intelligence.

Qualys

Qualys is a cloud-based security and compliance platform that helps organizations streamline security and compliance tasks. Qualys solutions cover areas such as vulnerability management, web application scanning, and policy compliance auditing. Cybersecurity Analysts may be asked about their experience with Qualys and other security tools used to detect and mitigate vulnerabilities.

Quantum cryptography

Quantum cryptography is a technique that uses the laws of quantum mechanics to secure communication channels. It relies on the fact that any attempts to measure or intercept a quantum message will introduce errors, alerting both parties to the presence of an eavesdropper. During an interview, you may be asked about your knowledge of quantum cryptography and its applications in securing communication channels.

Qubit

Qubit is a machine learning platform for the detection of security incidents. It uses machine learning algorithms to identify patterns of activity that could indicate an attack, and can also provide insights into the root cause of a security incident. During an interview, you may be asked about your experience working with machine learning platforms such as Qubit, or your insights into best practices when working with them.

Query

A query is a request for information from a database, which a Cybersecurity Analyst may use to uncover patterns or anomalies. During an interview, you may be asked about the various types of queries you're familiar with, such as SQL or NoSQL queries, and your experience with writing them. It's worth noting that knowledge of database management and querying is an essential skill for any Cybersecurity Analyst role.

QuickTime

QuickTime is a multimedia platform developed by Apple, which includes a media player, encoding and decoding tools, and other multimedia components. QuickTime has been a popular target for attacks, and Cybersecurity Analysts may be asked about their experience securing QuickTime components or dealing with vulnerabilities in the platform.

QWAC

A Qualified Website Authentication Certificate (QWAC) is a digital certificate used in the UK for secure online authentication. Cybersecurity Analysts may be asked about their experience with QWACs and other digital certificates, as well as their knowledge of best practices for managing and securing them.

Ransomware

A type of malware that encrypts a victim's files or systems and demands payment in exchange for the decryption key. Ransomware attacks can have severe consequences for individuals or organizations, including loss of data or system downtime.

Reconnaissance

In cybersecurity, reconnaissance refers to the initial phase of an attack where an attacker gathers information about the target system or organization. This can include identifying vulnerabilities, analyzing software and hardware configurations, and researching potential attack vectors.

Recovery Time Objective (RTO)

The maximum amount of time it takes for an organization's systems or services to be restored after a cyber attack or other disruption. The RTO is a critical metric for disaster recovery planning and helps organizations minimize the impact of an incident.

Red Team

A group of individuals who simulate an attacker or hacker to test an organization's security defenses. The red team aims to identify weaknesses and vulnerabilities that could be exploited by real attackers.

Remote Access

A method of accessing a computer or network from a remote location using a network connection. Remote access can be used for legitimate purposes, such as remote work or IT support, but can also be exploited by hackers as a potential attack vector. Cybersecurity analysts need to be familiar with potential security risks related to remote access and implement appropriate security controls to mitigate those risks.

Response Plan

A detailed plan of action that outlines the steps an organization must take in case of a cyber attack or security breach. It should include procedures for containing the attack, identifying the cause of the breach, and restoring systems to their previous state.

Reverse Engineering

The process of analyzing software or hardware to understand how it works and identify potential vulnerabilities or weaknesses. In a cybersecurity context, reverse engineering can help security professionals identify malware, and analyze potential security risks and attacks.

Risk Assessment

A process to identify, measure, and prioritize potential risks and threats to a system or organization. In a cybersecurity context, it involves evaluating the likelihood and impact of different cyber attacks and vulnerabilities, and developing strategies to mitigate those risks.

Risk Management

A process to identify, assess, and prioritize potential risks and threats to an organization, and develop strategies to mitigate or transfer those risks. Risk management in cybersecurity involves implementing security controls to reduce the likelihood and impact of cyber attacks.

Rootkit

A type of malware that can hide its presence from antivirus software and other security measures. Rootkits can grant an attacker unauthorized access to a system and allow them to control it remotely.

Sandbox

A virtual environment used for executing untested code, malware, or suspect data in a controlled manner without affecting the primary system. Cybersecurity Analysts use Sandbox to analyze the behavior of a malware and identify potential risks it poses to the system.

Scanning

The process of identifying vulnerabilities in a system by testing it for weaknesses. Cybersecurity Analysts use vulnerability scanners to identify security flaws and prioritize remediation efforts to reduce risk.

Security policy

A set of guidelines and procedures that define how an organization handles security. Cybersecurity Analysts develop and enforce security policies to protect against security threats and ensure compliance with legal and regulatory requirements.

SIEM

Security Information and Event Management. SIEM is a centralized platform that combines security event management (SEM) technologies with security information management (SIM). SIEM is commonly used by Cybersecurity Analysts to provide real-time analysis of security alerts generated by applications and network hardware.

Sniffing

The practice of capturing data packets transmitted over a network. Cybersecurity Analysts use sniffing tools to identify potential network security issues such as unauthorized access, malware, and data breaches.

SOC

Security Operations Center. A SOC is a dedicated facility within an organization that manages security and Cybersecurity operations. Cybersecurity Analysts work in a SOC to identify security threats, investigate security incidents, and respond to security breaches in real-time.

Social Engineering

The practice of manipulating people to reveal sensitive information or perform actions that compromise security. Cybersecurity Analysts educate employees on social engineering tactics and implement measures such as two-factor authentication and access controls to prevent social engineering attacks.

Spyware

Software designed to collect data from a computer or device without the user's knowledge or consent. Cybersecurity Analysts detect and remove spyware to prevent data theft or system compromise.

SQL injection

A technique used to exploit a vulnerability in a database-driven application by injecting malicious SQL code into the input field. This can lead to unauthorized data access or system compromise. Cybersecurity Analysts implement measures such as input validation and parameterized queries to prevent SQL injection attacks.

SSL

Secure Sockets Layer. SSL is the standard security protocol used to establish an encrypted link between a client and a server. Cybersecurity Analysts monitor SSL traffic to prevent cyber attacks such as man-in-the-middle attacks or data breaches.

Third-party Risk Management

The process of managing and assessing the risks associated with third-party suppliers such as vendors, contractors, and service providers. Third-party risk management is an essential component of cybersecurity as it helps to ensure that all parties involved in a project meet specific security standards and regulations. It also helps to detect and prevent cyber-attacks that may originate from third-party suppliers.

Threat Hunting

The proactive and iterative process of searching for signs of malicious activity that may have evaded traditional security systems. Threat hunting allows cybersecurity experts to identify potential threats and weaknesses in their systems and to develop proactive security measures against them. It is a critical component of a comprehensive cybersecurity strategy.

Threat Intelligence

A process of gathering and analyzing data to understand potential and current cybersecurity threats. It involves collecting data from various sources and analyzing it to detect patterns and identify potential risks before they unfold. Threat intelligence is critical for cybersecurity analysts as it helps them to develop proactive security measures against attacks from both internal and external sources.

Threat Modeling

A structured approach for identifying potential threats to a system or application. Threat modeling helps cybersecurity analysts to identify vulnerabilities and potential attack vectors and to develop proactive security measures to mitigate threats before they occur. Threat modeling typically involves four steps

Threat Surface

The sum total of all the points where a system or network is vulnerable to an attack. The threat surface includes all the components of a system, such as software applications, hardware, network connections, and user access. Cybersecurity analysts must be able to identify and assess the threat surface of a system to ensure that all potential vulnerabilities are addressed and any potential attacks are mitigated.

Tokenization

A process of converting sensitive data into non-sensitive data called tokens. Tokens are unique to a system and cannot be used to reconstruct the original data, making it much more difficult for hackers to steal. Tokenization is an effective way of protecting sensitive data, such as credit card numbers and social security numbers, and is used in industries such as healthcare and finance.

Traceability

A measure of how well a system's architecture, design, and implementation meet specific requirements. Traceability is crucial for cybersecurity analysts as it helps to ensure that the system's components meet specific security standards and regulations. It also enables experts to detect any deviations from the requirements and to develop a remediation plan effectively.

Traffic Analysis

The process of studying network traffic to identify malicious activity. Cybersecurity analysts use traffic analysis to detect and assess security threats, such as malware, viruses, and unauthorized access. Traffic analysis helps to identify potential weaknesses in the system and enables experts to develop proactive security measures against potential threats.

Trojan

A type of malware that disguises itself as a legitimate file or application to gain access to a system without the user's knowledge. Trojans can cause significant harm to a system and are often used in cyber espionage and data theft. Cybersecurity analysts must be able to detect and remove Trojan malware from systems and networks to prevent unauthorized access.

Two-Factor Authentication (2FA)

A security mechanism that requires users to provide two forms of identification before accessing a system or application. 2FA typically involves providing a password and then another form of identification, such as a fingerprint, smart card or biometric factor. This method significantly reduces the risk of unauthorized access and ensures that only the authorized user gains access to the system or application.

Unified Endpoint Management (UEM)

Refers to the security approach that provides a centralized platform for managing all endpoints, including desktops, laptops, smartphones, and tablets. This includes securing devices, monitoring access, and enforcing policies. Interviewers may ask how UEM solutions can help in securing endpoints.

Unified Threat Management (UTM)

Refers to the security approach that encompasses multiple security functions within a single solution. This could include firewall, antivirus, intrusion detection, web filtering, and virtual private network (VPN) capabilities. Interviewers may ask how an organization can benefit from the implementation of a UTM solution.

Unstructured Data

Refers to the data that is not organized in a specific format or structure, such as emails, social media posts, and documents. This data can be difficult to analyze and poses a challenge for cybersecurity analysts in identifying potential threats. Interviewers may ask how to secure unstructured data and how it differs from structured data.

Untrusted Networks

Refers to networks outside of an organization's control, such as public Wi-Fi networks. These networks can be a potential security risk as they provide easy access points for attackers. Interviewers may ask about the risks of using untrusted networks and how to protect against them.

Upstream Security

Refers to the security measures in place to protect data at its initial entry point into a network. This could include firewalls, intrusion prevention systems, and data loss prevention tools. Interviewers may ask about the importance of upstream security and the tools used to implement it.

URL Spoofing

Refers to the creation of a website that mimics a legitimate website, often used in phishing attacks. The spoofed website may have a similar design, domain name, or page structure to deceive users into entering personal information. Interviewers may ask how to identify and prevent URL spoofing attacks.

Use Case Analysis

Refers to the process of analyzing existing data to identify patterns and develop models that can be used to detect potential cybersecurity threats. Use case analysis helps cybersecurity analysts to identify potential weaknesses in their security strategy and take proactive measures to protect against them. Interviewers may ask how to perform a use case analysis and why it is important.

User Awareness Training

Refers to the training provided to employees to raise their awareness about cybersecurity threats and the best practices to avoid them. This includes social engineering attacks, phishing, and malware. Interviewers may ask about the benefits of user awareness training and the key topics that should be covered in such training sessions.

User Behavior Analytics (UBA)

Refers to the process of analyzing user activity data to identify patterns and anomalies that could be potential cybersecurity threats. UBA solutions use machine learning algorithms and statistical modeling to detect suspicious behavior and alert security teams. Interviewers may ask knowledge about UBA and how it helps in threat detection.

User Provisioning

Refers to the process of granting users access to an organization's IT resources. This process includes creating user accounts, assigning permissions, and setting up authentication methods. Interviewers may ask about the steps involved in user provisioning and how it relates to cybersecurity.

Virtual Patching

Virtual patching is a security measure used to protect against vulnerabilities before a permanent fix is available. It involves applying a temporary patch or workaround to mitigate the risk posed by an identified vulnerability. Cybersecurity Analysts should be familiar with virtual patching techniques and understand how to apply them to protect against known vulnerabilities.

Virtual Private Network (VPN)

A VPN provides a secure and private connection between two or more computer systems across an insecure public network, typically the internet. VPNs are commonly used to provide a secure connection for remote workers and to protect sensitive data during transmission. Cybersecurity Analysts need to understand the different types of VPNs, their strengths and weaknesses, and best practices for implementing and maintaining VPN connections.

Virus

A computer virus is a malicious program designed to replicate itself and spread from one computer system to another. Virus attacks can cause significant damage to computer systems and networks, leading to data loss, system crashes, and unauthorized access. As a Cybersecurity Analyst, it is essential to understand different types of viruses, how they propagate, and the techniques used to prevent and mitigate virus attacks.

Virus Signature

A virus signature is a unique set of characteristics or patterns that identify a virus or malware. Antivirus software uses these signatures to detect and remove viruses from computer systems. Cybersecurity Analysts should be knowledgeable in virus signature analysis, how to update antivirus software with the latest virus signatures, and other strategies to prevent viruses from infecting systems.

Voice over Internet Protocol (VoIP)

VoIP is a technology that enables voice communications over an IP network, such as the internet. VoIP can introduce unique security challenges, such as eavesdropping, spoofing, and denial-of-service attacks. Cybersecurity Analysts should be familiar with the risks associated with VoIP and the best practices for securing VoIP networks.

Voltage Control

Voltage control is a security measure used to protect against hardware-based attacks, such as fault injection or side-channel attacks. By controlling the voltage supplied to a device's processor, the likelihood of successful hardware-based attacks can be mitigated. Cybersecurity Analysts should be knowledgeable in voltage control techniques and understand how to implement voltage control measures to safeguard against hardware-based attacks.

VPN Concentrator

A VPN concentrator is a device that acts as a central point for managing VPN connections. It is a critical component of a corporate VPN infrastructure and manages the VPN tunnel endpoints, authenticates user credentials, and enforces security policies. Understanding the role and functionality of VPN concentrators is vital for Cybersecurity Analysts responsible for implementing or maintaining VPN connections.

Vulnerability Assessment

Refers to the process of identifying, analyzing, and prioritizing weaknesses in a computer system, network, or application that can potentially be exploited by cyber attackers. In an interview for a Cybersecurity Analyst position, understanding the techniques, tools, and methods used in vulnerability assessment is critical. This includes understanding how to conduct a vulnerability scan, interpret results, and recommend remediation measures to mitigate identified vulnerabilities.

Vulnerability Disclosure

Once a vulnerability has been identified, responsible disclosure helps to ensure that the necessary parties can take action to remediate the vulnerability before attackers can exploit it. Cybersecurity Analysts should be familiar with the responsible disclosure process, including how vulnerabilities are disclosed, who should be notified, and what actions should be taken to mitigate the vulnerability.

Vulnerability Management

Vulnerability management is a process that involves identifying, evaluating, prioritizing, and mitigating vulnerabilities in an organization's IT infrastructure. This process includes vulnerability assessment, patch management, and risk analysis. Cybersecurity Analysts should be familiar with the vulnerability management process and have a thorough understanding of the tools and methods used to ensure effective vulnerability management.

War Dialing

War Dialing is a technique used to scan phone numbers in order to find modems connected to the internet. The idea is to identify devices that are vulnerable to attacks such as brute-forcing.

Web Application Firewall (WAF)

A WAF is a type of firewall that is specifically designed to protect web applications. It is often used in conjunction with other security measures to prevent attacks such as SQL injections and cross-site scripting.

Web Application Penetration Testing

Web Application Penetration Testing is a type of security testing that is used to identify vulnerabilities and weaknesses within web applications. It involves simulating attacks against a web application in order to identify and report any security issues.

White Hat Hacker

A White Hat Hacker is an ethical hacker who uses their skills to identify and fix security vulnerabilities within an organization's IT infrastructure. They are often invited by companies to perform security audits in order to improve security measures.

Wireless Intrusion Detection System (WIDS)

A WIDS is a type of system that is used to detect unauthorized access to wireless networks. It is often used in large organizations to monitor Wi-Fi networks and alert administrators of any suspicious activity.

Wireless LAN Controller (WLC)

A WLC is a type of device that is used to manage wireless access points in a Wi-Fi network. It allows administrators to centrally manage security policies and settings, and provides a centralized view of the wireless network.

Wireshark

Wireshark is an open-source network analysis tool that captures packets and displays the information in a human-readable format. It is commonly used during a cybersecurity analyst interview to analyze network traffic and identify potential security threats.

Worm

A Worm is a type of malware that spreads itself autonomously through a computer network. It typically uses vulnerabilities in operating systems or applications to infect other devices on the network.

WPA (Wi-Fi Protected Access)

WPA is a type of wireless security protocol that is used to secure wireless networks. It is designed to be more secure than its predecessor, WEP (Wired Equivalent Privacy), and can be used with or without a pre-shared key (PSK).

WPA2

WPA2 is the second version of the Wi-Fi Protected Access protocol. It is an updated and more secure version of WPA that uses AES encryption to protect wireless networks.

YAML

Short for YAML Ain't Markup Language, is a human-readable data serialization format used for configuration files and data exchange. It is designed to be easy to read and write for both humans and machines, avoiding the complexity of modern markup languages.

YARA

A rule-based malware detection and classification tool that enables analysts to create and share custom rules to detect and classify malware. YARA rules allow analysts to identify specific patterns, behaviors, and attributes of malicious files, improving detection and response capabilities.

Yellow Teaming

A proactive approach where different teams (red and blue teams) collaborate to anticipate and prevent security threats. The yellow team plays the role of the adversary and the defender, simulating attacks and testing defenses. The goal is to improve overall security posture by identifying vulnerabilities and improving incident response plans.

YubiKey

A physical authentication device that generates one-time passwords and supports multi-factor authentication protocols such as Universal 2nd Factor (U2F) and Smart Card (PIV). It offers an extra layer of protection against phishing and other attacks, increasing the security of sensitive data and systems.